Take-Along Guide

Trees, Leaves and Bark

by Diane L. Burns

illustrations by Linda Garrow

NorthWord Press

Minnetonka, Minnesota

DEDICATION

To today's children, who care for tomorrow's trees

"I love all trees . . ."
—Aldo Leopold (naturalist)

ACKNOWLEDGMENTS

"The woods are lovely, dark and deep . . ."
—Robert Frost (poet)

And lovely also are the people who helped prepare this manuscript:
The staff of the Rhinelander District Library
D.N.R. forester Mike Beaufeaux
U.S. Forest Service silviculturist Dick Cutler
Dot Heintz and the UW-Extension 4-H program in Oneida County

Special thanks to:
Dan Krueger, Jr., professional horticulturist from
Northwoods Nursery, for his expertise.
Consolidated Paper Company forester Dan Hartman,
for his knowledge, patience, and meticulous help.

© Diane L. Burns, 1995

CREATIVE PUBLISHING international

NorthWord Press
5900 Green Oak Drive
Minnetonka, MN 55343
1-800-328-3895

Illustrations by Linda Garrow
Book design by Lisa Kronholm Moore

Library of Congress Cataloging-in-Publication Data
Burns, Diane L.
   Trees, leaves, and bark / by Diane L. Burns ; illustrations by Linda Garrow.
     p. cm. — (Take-along guide)
   ISBN 1-55971-628-2 (softcover)
   1. Trees—United States—Identification—Juvenile literature. 2. Leaves—
United States—Identification—Juvenile literature. 3. Bark—United
States—Identification—Juvenile literature.   I. Garrow, Linda. II. Title.
III. Series: Burns, Diane L. Take-along guide.
  QK475.B88   1995
  582.16—dc20   95-6695

Printed in Malaysia

CONTENTS
Trees, Leaves and Bark

INTRODUCTION

There are many kinds of trees all around us. They come in many sizes and shapes. This Take-Along Guide and its activities will help you know some of the trees that grow in prairies, woodlands, swamps and mountains across the United States.

TREES HAVE THREE PARTS

THE CROWN is the top of the tree where the branches, leaves, seeds and flowers are found.

THE TRUNK is the stem of the tree covered with bark to protect it. It holds the branches toward the sunlight. And it helps food travel between the roots and the branches.

THE ROOTS are the "underground branches" that pull up water and food for the tree from the soil. Roots hold the tree in place.

TREES CAN BE DIVIDED INTO TWO GROUPS

BROADLEAF trees have leaves that turn color and drop off for the winter. Their seeds grow inside fruits, nuts, pods or berries.

EVERGREEN or conifer trees have needles that stay green all year long. The seeds grow inside cones.

Have fun exploring and learning about Trees, Leaves and Bark.

ASPEN

TIPS TO FIND THIS TREE

Aspen seeds need sunlight to sprout; look for aspens in open areas.

They are the first broadleaf trees to spring up where land has been disturbed.

Listen for the leaves rustling in the breeze.

Aspens grow on open slopes of mountains.

LIFESPAN AND USES

Aspens grow to about 60 feet tall.

The wood is very soft. It makes good newspaper.

Aspens grow fast but only live about 60 years.

INTERESTING FACTS ABOUT ASPEN

Native Americans called this tree "noisy leaf."

Beavers love to eat aspen bark.

Bigtooth aspen and quaking aspen are the two kinds of aspen trees.

They grow throughout New England, the midwestern and western United States.

LEAVES

Aspen leaves are shiny and toothed. They are about the size of a silver dollar.

The leaf stems are flat.

On a branch, aspen leaves alternate like the teeth of a zipper.

BARK

Young aspen trees have smooth, pale green-white bark that looks shiny.

Full-grown trees have darker and rougher bark.

SEEDS

Caterpillar-like flowers become small hairy seeds.

The seeds blow away on the wind.

7

Tell someone where you are going and how long you will be gone.

WILLOW

TIPS TO FIND THIS TREE

Willows like it when their roots are wet. Look for willows along riverbanks and other wet edges.

In summer, look at the outline of the whole tree. Willow branches often bend toward the ground and wave gracefully in the breeze.

LIFESPAN AND USES

The willow is a short, sturdy tree that grows to 30-60 feet tall.

Willows are planted to keep soil from washing away; the tough roots hold soil against flooding.

Willow wood is soft and bends easily; it makes good toy whistles.

Willows live about 60 years.

INTERESTING FACTS ABOUT WILLOW

Willow bark can be made into aspirin.

There are 80 kinds of American willows. At least one kind grows in each of the 50 states.

LEAVES

Willow leaves are narrow and long, like green fingers.

Each leaf is 3-6 inches long, and they alternate along the branch like teeth of a zipper.

BARK

On young trees, willow bark is smooth and varies from red-brown to green-brown in color.

Grown trees have dark brown bark that is rough and has ridges.

SEEDS

Willow seeds are tiny, like poppy seeds.

These trees grow most easily from pieces of fallen twigs. New trees start wherever the twig lands.

Please treat all trees gently.

COTTONWOOD

TIPS TO FIND THIS TREE

Cottonwoods need sunlight to sprout. Look for them in open areas.

They also grow in dry areas anywhere water is found. Look along streams and creek bottomlands.

Sometimes, cottonwoods are planted for shade and windbreaks. You'll find them near farm and ranch houses.

In summer, use your ears to find cottonwoods. Listen for the rustling of the leaves.

LIFESPAN AND USES

Cottonwoods grow to about 100 feet tall.

The soft wood is made into newspaper.

The trees live more than 100 years.

INTERESTING FACTS ABOUT COTTONWOOD

Bees use the buds' sticky gum to seal cracks in their hives.

There are about a dozen types of cottonwoods in the United States. They grow across New England, the midwestern and western United States.

LEAVES

The shiny green, triangular leaves are 4-7 inches long.

Toothed cottonwood leaves have flat leaf stems.

The leaves alternate along the branch like the teeth of a zipper.

BARK

The bark is thin, smooth and pale gray on young trees.

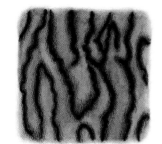

Older cottonwood bark is dark gray with deep, rounded ridges.

SEEDS

Cottonwoods have male and female trees.

On female trees, seed pods hang from strings. The ripe pods burst open with white fluffy "cotton."

Male cottonwoods have red, ropey flowers that look like fat caterpillars.

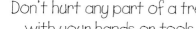

Don't hurt any part of a tree with your hands or tools.

11

JUNIPER

TIPS TO FIND THIS TREE

A juniper can be a scrubby, spreading tree. It can look like a low, prickly bush.

Junipers grow in soil with lots of rocks and sand.

Look in dry areas, too, where other trees cannot grow.

LIFESPAN AND USES

Junipers can grow up to 60 feet tall, but most are much shorter.

Its wood makes good campfires.

The berries are an important food for birds like waxwings, warblers and robins.

Junipers can live 300 years.

INTERESTING FACTS ABOUT JUNIPER

Native Americans used crushed juniper berries as an insect repellent.

There are more than a dozen kinds of junipers in the United States. They grow in the northeastern states, and also from Texas into the southwestern states and north into the Rocky Mountains.

LEAVES

Juniper leaves look like skinny green needles.

The leaves are small (less than half an inch long).

They lay flat against the twig and are rounded and scaly.

BARK

Often thin, scaly red-brown and rough, juniper bark feels shredded and soft.

SEEDS

Juniper seeds are hidden inside bluish berry-cones that are about the size of a pea.

Don't step on saplings
or bend them.

PAPER BIRCH

TIPS TO FIND THIS TREE

Look for the white bark of the trunk in the woods.

Paper Birches often grow in clumps of two or three trees.

In autumn, birch leaves turn bright yellow.

▶ DO NOT PEEL THE RAGGED BARK! It does not grow back.

LIFESPAN AND USES

Paper Birch trees grow quickly to their 60 foot height.

Birch wood is often used to make wooden spoons. It also makes a good campfire because it crackles as it burns, and it smells good.

To add beauty, birches are often planted in yards and town parks.

They live about 60 years.

INTERESTING FACTS ABOUT PAPER BIRCH

Paper Birch is nicknamed "canoe birch" because canoe frames were once covered with the tough, lightweight bark.

About a half-dozen kinds of birch trees grow in the northern United States, from coast to coast.

LEAVES

Birch leaves are egg-shaped, about 3 inches long.

They have pointed tips and thick teeth along the edge.

The leaves feel coarse.

Along the branch, the leaves alternate like the teeth of a zipper.

BARK

Paper Birch bark is smooth, chalk-white, and streaked with black.

The paper-thin bark may hang raggedly from the tree.

The inner bark is orange.

SEEDS

Many tiny winged seeds grow inside a narrow cone.

The cone is about as long as your thumb.

The seeds scatter on the winter winds.

Be aware of everything around you, especially changing weather.

SHAGBARK HICKORY

TIPS TO FIND THIS TREE

Hickories and oaks often grow next to each other.

Shagbark Hickory seeds need shade to sprout.

They grow up under other trees, never by themselves in an open field.

The leaves turn deep yellow in autumn.

LIFESPAN AND USES

Shagbark Hickories grow to be 100 feet tall.

Hard hickory wood makes strong handles for hammers and shovels, and dogsled runners.

Hickory nuts are an important wildlife food for squirrels and deer.

Hickory trees live about 250 years.

INTERESTING FACTS ABOUT SHAGBARK HICKORY

Small, tasty hickory nuts (about 100 to a pound) were important in Early American cooking.

Pioneers made a green dye for clothing from the bark.

The trees grow across the eastern half of the United States.

LEAVES

Shagbark Hickory leaflets are dark yellow-green and about 1 foot long.

They feel hairy on the edges.

There are 5 or 7 leaflets on a leaf. The end leaflet is larger than the others.

BARK

It is gray, and hangs in strips from the trunk.

It looks "shaggy," giving the tree its name.

SEEDS

These are nuts as small as your thumbnail.

They are hidden inside a thick, green husk.

Don't peel the bark, because that hurts the tree's growth.

MAPLE

TIPS TO FIND THIS TREE

Maples like moist, rich woods.

The seeds need shade to sprout.

In summer, look for the winged seeds that twirl to the ground.

In autumn, maple leaves turn shades of bright red and orange-yellow.

Maples are often planted for shade along city streets, in yards and town parks.

LIFESPAN AND USES

Maples grow to about 60 feet tall.

The wood of the maple tree is hard and tough. It makes good flooring for school gyms, and bowling pins.

Maples can live for 300 years or more.

INTERESTING FACTS ABOUT MAPLE

Maple leaves can be up to a foot long and wide.

Sap, a clear liquid that carries food up and down the trunk, can be boiled into maple syrup each spring.

One of a dozen kinds of maples can be found almost anywhere in the United States.

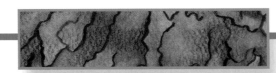

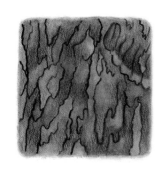

LEAVES

Maple leaves are hand-shaped, about as wide as they are tall.

The leaves grow opposite each other on the branch—"eye to eye."

BARK

Maple bark is silvery and smooth on young trees.

It is dark gray-brown with flaky grooves on older trees.

SEEDS

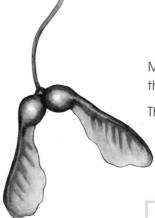

Maple seeds are winged, and look like the blades of a helicopter.

They drop off the tree in summer.

Don't put your hand into a hole or crack in the tree. It *may* be an animal's home.

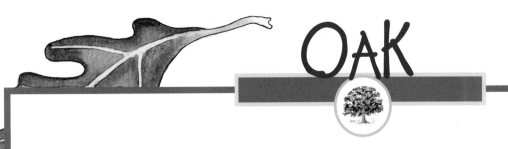

OAK

TIPS TO FIND THIS TREE

Oaks grow almost anywhere, some on drier ground, some on wetter.

In autumn, squirrels and blue jays are busy gathering oak nuts.

In winter, a few leaves cling to most oak branches and rattle in the wind.

LIFESPAN AND USES

Oaks grow from about 20-130 feet tall.

The beautiful, hard wood makes long-lasting furniture, like tables and chairs.

Acorns are important food for wild animals such as squirrels, raccoons and blue jays.

Oaks live from 200-500 years.

INTERESTING FACTS ABOUT OAK

Oak trees are divided into two groups, white oaks and black oaks.

Long ago, white oak nuts were ground into flour by Native Americans. Black oak nuts were too bitter.

A fully grown oak can make 50,000 acorns in one season. They would weigh a half ton!

Oaks grow all across the United States.

Don't leave behind any litter.

LEAVES

Oak leaves are taller than they are wide.

They have a leathery feel.

They have uneven shapes.

White oak leaves have rounded edges without teeth.

Black oak leaves have pointed edges and bristly teeth.

BARK

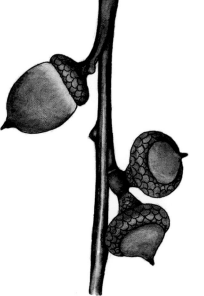

Oak bark is deeply ridged or flaky.

It can be gray-brown to dark brown in color.

SEEDS

Oak seeds are called acorns.

Acorns are brown, roundish nuts set inside a saucer-shaped cup.

EASTERN WHITE PINE

TIPS TO FIND THIS TREE

This pine grows on sandy, well-drained land.

The treetops have a soft, bushy look—like feathers.

▶ SPECIAL WARNING: Pitch on white pine cones and bark is sticky! It is hard to wash off hands and clothes

LIFESPAN AND USES

Eastern White Pines grow more than 100 feet tall.

The wood is often used for building houses.

These trees live about 400 years.

INTERESTING FACTS ABOUT EASTERN WHITE PINE

Pines are the largest group of conifers.

Long ago, Native Americans boiled white pine needles into a tea that soothed sore throats.

The Eastern White Pine is found throughout New England, southward into Virginia, North Carolina and Tennessee, then westward across the upper midwestern United States.

LEAVES

The soft, blue-green needles are about 4 inches long.

They grow in bundles of 5 needles.

BARK

Eastern White Pine bark is thin, smooth and green-gray on young trees.

It is thick, gray-brown and deeply grooved on older trees.

SEEDS

The cones are long and narrow, about 4-6 inches.

They are light brown and papery-feeling.

Globs of sticky pitch cling to the cones.

Stay away from poison ivy and poison oak.

MAKE A LEAF MOBILE

Use leaves from different trees for an interesting mobile.

THINGS YOU WILL NEED
▼

- assorted leaves (choose flat ones for the best results)
- 1 yard of clear contact paper
- 2 yards of thread, cut into 8 inch lengths
- 2 feet of yarn
- 1 toothpick
- 1 sturdy fallen branch about 12 inches long
- 1 pair of scissors
- clear tape

HERE'S HOW
▼

1 Cut two pieces of clear contact paper for each leaf. Make them a little larger than the leaf.

2 Peel the paper from the contact paper. Carefully lay each leaf onto the sticky side and cover it with another piece of peeled contact paper, sticky side down. Smooth out any air bubbles. Trim around the edges, using a scissors.

3 Poke a small hole near the top of each leaf, using the toothpick (but not too close to the top of the leaf or it will tear).

4 Pull a piece of thread through each hole.

5 Tie each leaf to the branch, anywhere. Tape in place.

6 Tie the yarn near the middle of the branch so that the mobile hangs straight and balanced.

Hang the leaf mobile from a hook in your ceiling.

MAKE A PINECONE SNACKBAR FOR BIRDS

Choose your pinecone on a dry day, or bring a wet cone inside and let it dry out before beginning.

THINGS YOU WILL NEED

▼

- 1 large, open pinecone
- 3 tablespoons of peanut butter
- 2 tablespoons of birdseed
- 1 tablespoon of ground-up bread crumbs
- 1 foot-long piece of thin wire bent into a hook at each end
- 1 sheet of newspaper
- 1 paper napkin

HERE'S HOW

▼

1 Spread the newspaper over your workspace to catch any spills.

2 Smear peanut butter over the pinecone's edges and into its cracks, using your fingers. Wipe your hands clean on the napkin.

3 Sprinkle birdseed and bread crumbs over the peanut butter, pressing to keep it in place.

4 Loop the hooked end of the wire around the top of the pinecone, twisting it tightly so it won't come loose.

5 Hang the snackbar on a branch outside.

Then, watch from indoors as the birds enjoy your feast.

In dry weather, the scales open to release the seeds. In damp weather, the scales close to keep the seeds dry. To make this snackbar, the scales *must* be open.

25

AMERICAN SYCAMORE

TIPS TO FIND THIS TREE

Sycamores need much moisture.

Look for them in wet bottomlands.

Watch for the white, patchy look of the trunk.

Sycamore crowns are round and wide.

LIFESPAN AND USES

American Sycamore trees grow to about 100 feet tall.

Its wood makes boxes for shipping things like fruits and vegetables.

The sycamore lives about 500 years.

INTERESTING FACTS ABOUT AMERICAN SYCAMORE

American Sycamores are native to the United States. They grow in the eastern part, and in the streambanks and valleys of the south-western states.

Sycamores grow the widest trunks of any American tree: up to 14 feet!

LEAVES

Sycamore leaves are big—up to 10 inches wide.

Each leaf has 3-5 lobes. The undersides are hairy.

Each leaf is shiny green on top and pale green underneath.

BARK

The sycamore's flat gray bark does not stretch as the trunk grows.

Patches of bark peel off and leave behind bare, white spots.

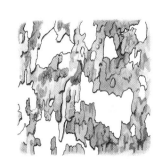

SEEDS

A solid, spiky-looking ball covers the seeds.

It hangs on the tree all winter.

It is about the size of a golfball.

Don't approach or touch any plants you don't know.

ASH

TIPS TO FIND THIS TREE

Most ash trees in the eastern United States grow in moist places.

Ash seeds drop off in late autumn.

The crown is tall and oval.

LIFESPAN AND USES

Ash trees grow to about 70 feet tall.

Strong, springy ash wood makes sporting goods such as baseball bats and snowshoes.

Ash trees live about 100 years.

INTERESTING FACTS ABOUT ASH

It was once believed that ash trees cured sick children when they passed under the branches.

More than a dozen kinds of ash trees grow in the United States. They are found from the east coast, into the southern states and across the plains states.

LEAVES

These leaves have 7 or 9 leaflets with a few blunt teeth along the edges.

The leaflets are about 10 inches long.

The leaves grow in opposite pairs along the branch.

BARK

Ash bark is grayish.

Its ridges form a diamond shape.

SEEDS

The seeds have slender wings like the blades of a helicopter.

They droop in clusters about 2 inches long.

Don't push against dead tree trunks. They can snap off and hurt you.

EASTERN LARCH

TIPS TO FIND THIS TREE

Wear boots! The larch grows on wet, swampy ground.

Eastern Larches are easiest to find in autumn when their needles turn a soft yellow color.

They often grow close together with slender trunks and skinny branches.

LIFESPAN AND USES

Larches are straight trees that may grow to 60-75 feet tall.

Its wood is used to make newspaper and fenceposts.

A larch may live to be 200 years old.

INTERESTING FACTS ABOUT EASTERN LARCH

Unlike other conifers, the eastern larch sheds its needles each fall.

Larches grow from the Ohio River Valley north all the way to the Arctic, where a fully grown tree may be only several feet tall.

"Tamarack" is a Native American name for the larch.

LEAVES

Larches have soft needles about an inch long.

They grow in bundles of about a dozen needles.

BARK

Eastern Larch bark is scaly and rough.

It is red-brown in color.

SEEDS

Seeds of the larch tree grow inside small, round cones.

The cones, less than 1 inch long, face upward on the branches.

New cones are greenish and grow at the tip of the branch.

Old cones are brown and grow farther back on the branch.

Don't approach or touch any wild animals you might see.

NORTHERN WHITE-CEDAR

TIPS TO FIND THIS TREE

This tree likes wet places.

It often grows by itself.

It has a compact, triangular shape.

LIFESPAN AND USES

Northern White-cedar grows to about 50 feet tall.

The wood does not rot, so it is used for making roof shingles.

White-cedar is also an important deer food in winter.

These trees live more than 300 years.

INTERESTING FACTS ABOUT NORTHERN WHITE-CEDAR

This tree is also known as Arbor Vitae, which means "tree of life."

It was probably the first American tree carried back to Europe by French explorers.

Northern White-cedar grows in the very north-eastern states, into the Great Lakes region, and Virginia, North Carolina and Tennessee.

LEAVES

White-cedar leaves are scale-like and lay flat along the branch.

They are about one-quarter inch long.

They are smooth and dull green.

BARK

White-cedar bark is thin, and gray to red-brown.

It hangs in soft, skinny shredded strips.

SEEDS

White-cedar cones are small, less than one-half inch long.

They are yellow-brown and egg-shaped.

The cones hang either in clusters or alone.

Get permission before going onto someone's land.

LODGEPOLE PINE

TIPS TO FIND THIS TREE

The tree grows slender, leggy trunks on lower ground.

High on the mountain, weather twists and bends its shape.

LIFESPAN AND USES

Lodgepole Pines can grow to about 70 feet tall.

The wood is used for rustic fenceposts around homes and corrals.

This tree lives about 250 years.

INTERESTING FACTS ABOUT LODGEPOLE PINE

The lodgepole pine's slender trunks were used as frames for Native American lodges. The tree was named after them.

Lodgepoles grow from sea level to mountaintop in the western states.

LEAVES

Lodgepole needles are about 2 inches long.

They grow in pairs and look twisted.

They are bright yellow-green.

BARK

Lodgepole bark is pale brown and only about 1 inch thick.

It is made of thin, small scales.

SEEDS

Lodgepole seeds grow inside cones that are shiny yellow-brown.

The cones are less than 2 inches long and grow in clusters.

On the cones, each scale has a slender prickle.

Watch where you step.

PONDEROSA PINE

TIPS TO FIND THIS TREE

Look for the red-orange bark.

Ponderosa Pines have a narrow, tall shape.

They have a feathery-soft look at the top.

LIFESPAN AND USES

They grow to about 200 feet tall.

Ponderosa Pine wood is used to make parts of houses, like the window frames.

Ponderosa Pine trees live as long as 500 years.

INTERESTING FACTS ABOUT PONDEROSA PINE

Ponderosa Pine is also known as Western Yellow Pine.

Explorers Lewis and Clark wrote about it in 1804 on their famous journey out West.

The name "ponderosa" means "massive."

Ponderosa Pines grow on dry uplands of the western and southwestern United States and the plains states.

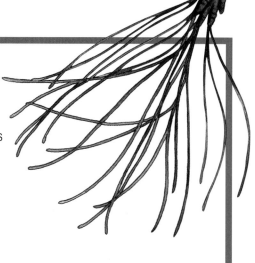

LEAVES

Yellow-green ponderosa pine needles grow in bundles of 2 or 3.

They are 4-11 inches long.

BARK

Trees younger than 100 years have bark that is nearly black in color.

Trees older than 100 years have bright red-orange bark.

It is formed in large flaky plates with black lines in between.

The flaky plates look like puzzle pieces.

SEEDS

Ponderosa seeds grow inside cones that are 3-5 inches long.

The cones have a prickly hook on each scale.

First-year cones are green. They sit upright on the branch.

Second-year cones turn brown and hang down to spill the seeds.

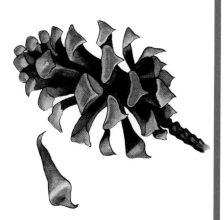

Wear boots and other appropriate clothing.

37

DOUGLAS FIR

TIPS TO FIND THIS TREE

The treetops have a pointy shape.

Look for the deep grooves in the bark.

LIFESPAN AND USES

Douglas Fir trees can grow to 300 feet tall.

The strong wood is used for building houses.

Young trees make very good Christmas trees.

Douglas Fir trees can live for more than 1,000 years!

INTERESTING FACTS ABOUT DOUGLAS FIR

The bark on these fully grown trees can be a foot thick!

Next to the redwoods, Douglas Fir is the tallest tree in the United States.

Douglas Fir trees grow throughout the western and southwestern United States on drier uplands from sea level up to 9,000 feet.

Take your time and don't hurry.

LEAVES

The flat, short needles are about 1 inch long.

The single needles grow all around the branch.

The needles are dark green in color.

BARK

Douglas Fir bark is thick and red-brown.

It has deep grooves.

SEEDS

Douglas Fir cones hang down.

The cones are reddish and 2-4 inches long.

The cones have three-pronged "tongues" that stick out between the scales.

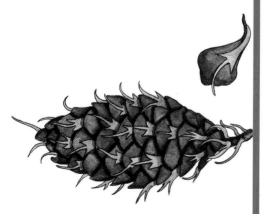

39

GROW YOUR OWN TREE

In spring, summer, or autumn, you can plant the young tree outside.

THINGS YOU WILL NEED

▼

- Any closed pine cone, dark in color
- 2 clean, empty 8-ounce yogurt cartons with drain holes poked in the bottom and filled with good garden soil
- 2 waterproof saucers
- 1 paper plate

HERE'S HOW

▼

1 Keep the closed pinecone in a warm, dry place until it opens.

2 Shake the seeds from the pinecone over the paper plate.

3 Choose 2 seeds that are dark in color. (Light-colored seeds will not grow).

4 Plant each of the seeds in its own yogurt cup by pressing lightly into the soil so it is covered.

5 Put the cup on a waterproof saucer in a sunny place.

6 Every few days, water the cup carefully so that the soil is moist, not soggy.

Be sure to leave room around the tree so it isn't crowded.

Water it when it gets dry.

Be patient! Trees grow very slowly.

MAKE A BARK RUBBING POSTER

To make a "bark art" collection, use rubbings from several different trees.

THINGS YOU WILL NEED

▼

- Thin drawing paper, such as onion skin or tracing paper
- 4 thumbtacks
- Assorted crayon stubs with the paper peeled off
- Any mature trees with healthy bark

HERE'S HOW

▼

1 Use thumbtacks to pin a piece of paper against the tree trunk at eye level.

2 Rub the flat length of the crayon across the paper.

3 Change the crayon color as often as you like.

4 As you rub, the pattern of the bark will appear.

5 Hang your poster where everyone can admire it.

Bark can be hurt, so thumbtack your paper just deep enough to hold it in place.

When you are done, be sure to remove the thumbtacks and take them home with you.

41

SCRAPBOOK

Trees, Leaves and Bark